Remembrance Journal

A prompting journal for the grieving soul.

Cathleen Groteluschen

An Everly After Book

Copyright © 2020 by Cathleen Groteluschen
Title: Remembrance Journal / Cathleen Groteluschen
Description: First Edition | Nebraska | Everly After, 2020
Contact: everlyafter.net

First Edition, April 2020
ISBN: 978-1-952226-01-4 (Paperback, USA)
ISBN: 978-1-95226-02-1 (Leathered Hardback)

Cover Art & Design by Evgenia Dolotovskaia
Format Design by Evgenia Dolotovskaia

Printed in the United States of America.

A journal that I dedicate to you ———————————————————

Your memory will live on as I cherish you.

Picture of you

You will forever and always hold a place in my heart.

Picture of us

Remembering You

Your Name

_____

_____

Your Birthdate

_____

_____

You passed away on

_____

_____

You are my

_____

_____

_____

Your living relatives are

_____

_____

_____

In heaven you are joining

_____

_____

_____

_____

My prayer for you is ...

When someone you love becomes a memory,
the memory becomes a treasure.
- Author Unknown -

What I love about you ...

How lucky I am to have something that
makes saying goodbye so hard.
- Winnie The Pooh -

I am always going to remember you by ...

A limb has fallen from the family tree
that says grieve not for me. Remember
the best times, the laughter, the song,
the good life I lived while I was strong.
- Author Unknown -

Since you have left I watch over ...

You never know how strong you are,
until being strong is the only choice you have.
- Bob Marley -

I want people to know that you were ...

No one is actually dead until the ripples
they cause in the world die away.
- Terry Pratchett -

Your bodily features included ...

*Beautiful memories silently kept of one
that we loved and will never forget.*
- Author Unknown -

My favorite look of yours …

Just when the caterpillar thought the world was over,
it became a butterfly.
- Chuang Tzu -

I remember how you would dress ...

From day to day, I frequently find,
images of you going through my mind.
- Author Unknown -

Your personality was …

If only our eyes saw souls instead of bodies
how very different our ideals of beauty would be.
- Author Unknown -

I would describe you as ...

Be the things you loved most about the people that are gone.
- Author Unknown -

I liked to call you ...
I would call you that because ...

_____

_____

_____

_____

_____

_____

_____

_____

_____

_____

_____

_____

_____

_____

_____

_____

_____

_____

I wrote your name in the sky, but the wind blew it away.
I wrote your name in the sand, but the waves washed it away.
I wrote your name in my heart, and forever it will stay.
- Jessica Blade -

You liked to call me ...
You would call me that because ...

Goodbyes are not forever. Goodbyes are not the end.
They simply mean I'll miss you, until we meet again!
- Author Unknown -

We met by …

Words can't wipe away your tears.
Hugs won't ease your pain, but hold on to your memories.
Forever they'll remain.
- Author Unknown -

We new each other for …

I can go days without talking to you, months without seeing you,
but not a second goes by that I'm not thinking about you.
- Anurag Prakash Ray -

Your best friend ...

Love is just a word until someone comes along and gives it meaning.
- Paulo Coelho -

Animals that you loved ...

Those we love and lose are always connected by heartstrings into infinity.
- Terri Guillemets -

Some of your hobbies included ...

The trouble is, you think you have time.
- Buddha -

Favorite sports of yours included ...

You may be gone from my sight,
but you are never gone from my heart.
- Winnie The Pooh -

In your time of leisure you would …

God doesn't call the qualified.
He qualifies the called.
- Christine Caine -

You were happiest when ...

Those we love never truly leave us.
There are things that death cannot touch.
- Jack Thorne -

Our favorite routine together was ...

We love them. We miss them. We grieve them.
And so, we live our lives to make them proud.
- Author Unknown -

You would talk about the day we spent ...

Think only of the past as its remembrance gives you pleasure.
- Jane Austen -

The music you enjoyed …

Sometimes it only takes one song to bring back a thousand memories.
- Author Unknown -

Your favorite movie ...

Somewhere over the rainbow, skies are blue,
and the dreams that you dare to dream really do come true.
- Judy Garland -

You liked to collect ...

Collect things you love, that are authentic to you,
and your house becomes your story.
- Erin Flett -

Your most prized possession ...

Wherever a beautiful soul has been there is a trail of beautiful memories.
- Ronald Reagan -

One of your favorite stories to tell ...

I think I'll miss you forever like the stars
miss the sun in the morning skies.
- Lana Del Rey -

You were always so good at …

What we have once enjoyed we can never lose.
All that we love deeply becomes a part of us.
- Helen Keller -

I remember you to be motivated by ...

A life that touches others goes on forever.
- Author Unknown -

Someone that you considered a hero was ...

*A hero is an ordinary individual who finds the strength
to persevere and endure in spite of overwhelming obstacles.*
- Christopher Reeve -

One time you payed it forward by ...

The purpose of human life is to serve,
and to show compassion and the will to help others.
- Albert Schweitzer -

On the weekends you would ...

*Enjoy the little things in life, because one day
you will look back and realize they were the big things.*
- Kurt Vonnegut -

Your favorite season ...

I hope I can be the Autumn leaf, who looked at the sky and lived.
And when it was time to leave, gracefully it knew life was a gift.
- Dodinsky -

I remember you to be so grateful for ...

It is not length of life, but depth of life.
- Ralph Waldo Emerson -

Your favorite holiday was ...

When someone we love is in heaven, a
little bit of heaven is in our home.
- Author Unknown -

Traditions you carried on during the holiday seasons ...

*Remembrance is the only paradise out
of which we cannot be driven away.*
- Charles Francis Richter -

Your favorite thing to eat ...

The secret of a good life is to have the right loyalties
and hold them in the right scale of values.
- Norman Thomas -

When we went out you would always order ...

Food brings people together on many different levels.
It's nourishment of the soul and body; it's truly love.
- Giada De Laurentiis -

Places you traveled ...

Life is meant for spectacular adventures.
Let your feet wander, your eyes marvel, and your soul ignite.
- Author Unknown -

You loved spending time with ...

True love stories never have endings.
- Richard Bach -

Your dream in life was …

_____

_____

_____

_____

_____

_____

_____

_____

_____

_____

_____

_____

_____

_____

_____

_____

_____

_____

_____

_____

_____

Change is the essence of life; be willing
to surrender what you are for what you could become.
- Reinhold Niebuhr -

In your life time you accomplished ...

Don't cry because it's over, smile
because it happened.
- Dr. Seuss -

How you earned money was by ...

*There are two educations. One should teach us how to
make a living and the other how to live.*
- John Adams -

So much in life you overcame ...

It has to be hard so you'll never ever forget.
- Bob Harper -

Your values included ...

May every sunrise hold more promise,
every moonrise hold more peace.
- Author Unknown -

The best advice you gave to me ...

*We all die. The goal isn't to live forever,
the goal is to create something that will.*
- Chuck Palahniuk -

You taught me to be ...

*Courage doesn't always roar. Sometimes courage is the quiet voice
at the end of the day saying, 'I will try again tomorrow.'*
- Mary Anne Radmacher -

Something you would find comfort in ...

Seeing death as the end of life is like
seeing the horizon as the end of the ocean.
- David Searls -

Things that would make you so happy are ...

Life isn't worth living until you
have found something worth dying for.
- Martin Luther King, Jr. -

Things that could make you so sad were ...

Keep your face to the sunshine and you
cannot see a shadow.
- Helen Keller -

The love you had in your eyes for ...

*There are some who bring a light so great to the world
that even after they have gone, the light remains.*
Author Unknown -

You were always so interesting ...

Loved with a love beyond all feelings,
missed with a grief beyond all tears.
- Author Unknown -

Once you told me …

I have told you these things, so that in me you may have peace.
In this world you will have trouble.
But take heart! I have overcome the world.
- John 16:33 -

I remember the time you ...

If there ever comes a day when we can't be together,
keep me in your heart, I'll stay there forever.
- Winnie The Pooh -

We shared in the laughter …

You don't stop laughing because you grow older.
You grow older because you stop laughing.
- Maurice Chevalier -

You would show me you cared by ...

A heart is not judged by how much you
love, but by how much you are loved by others.
- The Wizard of Oz -

The way you expressed love was ...

Beyond this vale of tears there is a life above.
Unmeasured by the flight of years; and all that life is love.
- James Montgomery -

You were most passionate about ...

*In life you can either follow your fears
or be led by your values, by your passions.*
- William Sloane Coffin -

Your spiritual life consisted of ...

For we walk by faith, not by sight.
- 2 Corinthians 5:7 -

*Something not many people
would know about you ...*

No one outside ourselves can rule us
inwardly. When we know this, we become free.
- Buddha -

Always you would use the word ...

What cannot be said will be wept.
- Sappho -

A motto of yours …

To pray is to let go and let God take over.
- Philippians 4:6-7 -

I laugh when I remember the time you ...

That it will never come again
is what makes life so sweet.
- Emily Dickinson -

Often you talked about …

Sometimes I just look up, smile and say,
"I know that was you. Thank you."
- Author Unknown -

A pet peeve of yours was …

Some things in life cannot be fixed.
They can only be carried.
- Megan Devine -

My favorite memory of us …

*Memories of our lives, of our works and
our deeds will continue in others.*
- Rosa Parks -

A special thing you did for me ...

Something tells me I'm going to love you forever.
- Unknown Author -

You always made me feel ...

What is the difference between "I like you" and "I love you"?
When you like a flower, you just pluck it.
But when you love a flower, you water it daily.
One who understands this, understands life.
- Buddha -

One time we both …

To live in hearts we leave behind is not to die.
- Thomas Campbell -

A time you became embarrassed ...

While we are mourning the loss of our friend,
others are rejoicing to meet him behind the veil.
- John Taylor -

The best gift you ever gave me was ...

When you are sorrowful, look again in your heart,
and you shall see that in truth you are weeping
for that which has been your delight.
- Kahlil Gibran -

We were so proud when …

May there be comfort in knowing that
someone so special will never be forgotten.
- Julie Hebert -

You taught me most about ...

Death is not the opposite of life, but a part of it.
- Haruki Murakami -

Together we accomplished ...

Coming together is a beginning,
staying together is progress,
and working together is success.
- Henry Ford -

A poem I dedicate to you ...

Walk on, walk on with hope in your heart,
and you'll never walk alone, you'll never walk alone.
- Oscar Hammerstein II -

Together we shared ...

I miss you more every day and even though I am one day closer
to the day we meet again, I miss you all the same.
- Author Unknown -

You would tease me about ...

Do what makes you happy, be with those who make you smile,
and laugh as much as you breathe.
- Author Unknown -

You left me with ...

God will give you the power to have
peace in the midst of the storm.
- Joyce Meyer -

You saved me from ...

Tears are prayers too.
They travel to God when we can't speak.
- Psalm 56:8 -

In life you did not deserve ...

There are only two ways to live your life.
One is as though nothing is a miracle.
The other is as though everything is a miracle.
- Albert Einstein -

If I could take just one thing back ...

Never regret anything. Because every little detail of your life
is what made you into who you are in the end.
- Drew Barrymore -

If you could do something differently ...

*Perhaps the butterfly is proof that you can go through
a great deal of darkness, yet become something beautiful.*
- Beau Taplin -

Together in life we treasured ...

The most treasured gifts are the wonderful moments
we create with the people we love.
They become priceless memories decorating our lives.
- Dodinsky -

The day you passed …

Life and death are one thread,
the same line viewed from different sides.
- Lao Tzu -

We celebrated your life by ...

Better than I was, more than I am.
And all of this happened by taking your hand.
- Tim McGraw -

You were laid to rest …

Now you are in a better place. Your soul is laid to rest.
Safe with all the angels, for they only take the best.
- Author Unknown -

Those who came to celebrate you ...

You will always be in my heart
because in there you're still alive.
- Jamie Cirello -

We honored you in many ways ...

Honor me not by mourning my death,
but by celebrating my life.
- Chris M. Braden -

You would love most about your celebration of life ...

Grief is like the ocean; it comes in waves; ebbing and flowing.
Sometimes the water is calm, and sometimes it is overwhelming.
All we can do is learn to swim.
- Vicki Harrison -

My keepsake from the celebration of life ...

And in the end it's not the years in your life that count;
it's the life in your years.
- Abraham Lincoln -

Your legacy lives on through ...

The loss is immeasurable,
but so is the love left behind.
- Author Unknown -

If we could spend another day together we would ...

We only part to meet again.
- John Gay -

I want to tell you one more thing ...

*Strength grows in the moments when you think
you can't go on but you keep going anyway.*
- Author Unknown -

Every time I hear this I will think of you ...

You're probably looking down from heaven up above,
sending out smiles with days of sunshine and showers of love.
- Napua -

My letter to you …

Grief never ends, but it changes. It is a passage, not a place to stay.
Grief is not a sign of weakness, nor a lack of faith. It is the price of love.
- Author Unknown -

Made in the USA
Coppell, TX
04 September 2021